THE PRAYER THAT JESUS TAUGHT US: *OUR FATHER*

Fr. Ugo Vanni

Preface by Pope Francis

NOTES ON PRAYER

Volume 8

Our Sunday Visitor
Huntington, Indiana

Palazzo San Pio X, Via della Conciliazione, 5 00120 Città del Vaticano
www.pcpne.va; www.iubilaeum2025.va
Published 2024 by Our Sunday Visitor, Inc.

Our Sunday Visitor Publishing Division
Our Sunday Visitor, Inc.
200 Noll Plaza
Huntington, IN 46750
1-800-348-2440

ISBN: 978-1-63966-282-1 (Inventory No. T2943)
eISBN: 978-1-63966-283-8
LCCN: 2024948666

Cover and interior design: Amanda Falk
Cover art: Adobestock

OSV extends thanks to the Catholc Truth Society for its collaboration in producing this book.

Printed in the United States of America

Contents

Preface by Pope Francis

Prayer is the breath of faith, its most proper expression. It's like a silent cry that comes out from the heart of whoever trusts and believes in God. It's not easy to find words to express this mystery. How many definitions of prayer we can gather from the saints and masters of spirituality, as well as from the reflections of theologians! Nevertheless, it is always and only in the simplicity of those who live prayer that prayer finds expression. The Lord, moreover, warned us that, when we pray, we must not waste words, deluding ourselves that thus we will be heard. He taught us rather to prefer silence and to entrust ourselves to the Father, who knows the kind of things we need even before we ask for them (see Mt 6:7–8).

The Ordinary Jubilee of 2025 is already at the door. How to prepare ourselves for this event, so important for the life of the Church, if not by means of prayer? The year 2023 was set aside for a rediscovery of the conciliar teachings, contained especially in the four constitutions of the Second Vatican Council. It is a way of keeping alive the mandate that the Fathers gathered at the council wished to place in our hands, so that by means of its implementation, the Church might recover its youthful face and proclaim, in a language adapted to the men and women of our time, the beauty of the Faith.

Now is the time to prepare for a year that will be dedicated entirely to prayer. In our own time the need is being felt more and more strongly for a true spirituality capable of responding to the great questions which confront us every day of our lives, questions caused by a global scenario that is far from serene. The ecological-economic-social crisis aggravated by the recent pandemic; wars, especially the one in Ukraine, which sow death, destruction, and poverty; the culture of indifference and waste that tends to stifle aspirations for peace and solidarity and keeps God at the margins of personal and social life. … These phenomena combine to bring about a ponderous atmosphere that holds many people back from living with joy and serenity. What we need, therefore, is that our prayer should rise up with greater insistence to the Father so that he will listen to the voice of those who turn to him, confident of being heard.

This year dedicated to prayer is in no way intended to affect the initiatives which every particular Church considers it must plan for in its own daily pastoral commitment. On the contrary, it aims to recall the foundation on which the various pastoral plans should be developed and find consistency. This is a time when, as individuals or communities, we can rediscover the joy of praying in a variety of forms and expressions. A time of consequence enabling us to increase the certainty of our faith and trust in the intercession of the Virgin Mary and the saints. In short, a year in which we can have the experience almost of a "school of prayer," without taking anything for granted (or at cut-rate), especially with regard to our way of praying, but making our own, every day, the words of the disciples when they asked Jesus: "Lord, teach us to pray" (Lk 11:1).

In this year we are invited to become more humble and to leave space for the prayer that flows from the Holy Spirit. It is he who knows how to put into our hearts and onto our lips the right words so that we will be heard by the Father. Prayer in the Holy Spirit is what unites us with Jesus and allows us to adhere to the will of the Father. The Spirit is the interior Teacher who indicates the way to follow. Thanks to him the prayer of even just one person can become the prayer of the entire Church, and vice versa. There is nothing like prayer according to the Spirit to make Christians feel united as the one family of God. It is God who knows how to recognize everyone's needs and how to make those needs become the invocation and intercession of all.

I am certain that bishops, priests, deacons, and catechists will find more effective ways this year of placing prayer as the basis of the announcement of hope which the 2025 Jubilee intends to make resonate in this troubled time. For this reason, the contribution of consecrated persons will be of great value, particularly communities of contemplative life. I hope that in all the shrines of the world, privileged places for prayer, initiatives should be increased so that every pilgrim can find an oasis of serenity and return with a heart filled with consolation. May prayer, both personal and communal, be unceasing, without interruption, according to the will of the Lord Jesus (see Lk 18:1), so that the kingdom of God may spread, and the Gospel reach every person seeking love and forgiveness.

As an aid for this Year of Prayer, some short texts have been produced which, with their simple language, will make possible entry into the various dimensions of prayer. I thank the authors for their contribution and willingly place into your hands these "notes" so that everyone can rediscover the beauty of trusting in the Lord with humility and joy. And don't forget to pray also for me.

Vatican City
September 27, 2023

Franciscus

Foreword

> For whatever other words we may say — whether the desire of the person praying go before the words, and employ them in order to give definite form to its [the prayer's] requests, or come after them, and concentrate attention upon them, that it may increase in fervor — if we pray rightly, and as becomes our wants, we say nothing but what is already contained in the Lord's Prayer. And whoever says in prayer anything which cannot find its place in that gospel prayer, is praying in a way which, if it be not unlawful, is at least not spiritual; and I know not how carnal prayers can be lawful, since it becomes those who are born again by the Spirit to pray in no other way than spiritually.

These words of Saint Augustine (*Letter 130*, 12, 22) allow us to grasp the profound meaning of the prayer of the *Our Father*. Jesus could not have imparted to his disciples any prayer other than this, a synthesis of his entire Gospel. Over the centuries the Church has referred to it in various ways: "Prayer of the Lord's Day," "the Lord's Prayer." For Christians, it remains simply the *Our Father*, the prayer that Jesus himself has taught us. Far from any formula, here lies the heart of the relationship with God and what the Christian experiences in the depths of his heart. This is the prayer of the individual believer and of the whole Church, which experiences in this way the perennial presence of the life-giving Spirit.

It is no accident that the first text after the writings of the New Testament, the Didaché, should dwell on the *Our Father*, instructing the first believers that this prayer is to be recited "three times a day" (VIII, 2). In its catechetical simplicity, the book highlights that in the crucial moments that mark the Christian's day, the *Our Father* remains the essential point of reference.

As we know, Pope Francis has asked that the year immediately preceding the Ordinary Jubilee of 2025 be dedicated to prayer. This has led among other things to the creation of a simple series, entitled "Notes on Prayer" to indicate that speech or writing about prayer can only outline some of its aspects. The mystery of prayer endures, the cargo deep within it proving unfathomable. After all, who could presume to exhaust the essence of prayer, which always remains a privileged action of the Holy Spirit who comes to the aid of each one's weakness, as the apostle reminds us (cf. Rom 8:26)?

Among these "Notes," a text introducing the *Our*

Father could not be left out. There are many commentaries on the Lord's Prayer, and they span the two thousand years of our history. From Tertullian to Pope Francis, it is possible to produce an extensive review that highlights the permanent interest in this prayer, which persists in its uniqueness. I chose the text that in his day I had asked of a friend and colleague, Fr. Ugo Vanni to write. I remember the circumstances perfectly. I had been tasked with preparing a commentary on the *Catechism of the Catholic Church* that would be published within a few months. The congregation for doctrine had sent me the drafts of the text in its first French edition. In a few days I managed to put together a team of professors, most of them colleagues from the Gregorian, who immediately went to work.

I also knocked on the door of Fr. Vanni, who welcomed me with his good-natured and sincere smile. Fr. Ugo was a true man of God. A profound teacher and a very fatherly priest. He knew how to convey fellow feeling and trust in a natural manner, without pretense or clerical attitudes. He possessed a humanity that allowed his goodness to shine through, and lived a spirituality that opened the hearts of those who turned to him for sure guidance. I asked Fr. Vanni if he could write a commentary on the *Our Father*, the last chapter of the *Catechism*. The look he gave me was one of surprise. Then he said, "Don Rino, if it's you that's asking, I can't say no … but I'll confess that it's quite a challenge."

So it was that Fr. Vanni wrote his beautiful commentary on the *Our Father*. He managed to combine exegesis with original interpretation in such a way that it still remains relevant today. As editor I took the liberty of adjusting the text to adapt it to the series, making it shorter, tighter and easier to read. Nothing is changed in the thought or writing of Fr. Vanni, whom as a friend I still remember in prayer. The publication of this text is meant first and foremost as a sign of acknowledgment of his fruitful pastoral ministry, along with the desire to keep the memory of his teaching alive.

The *Our Father*, as the *Catechism of the Catholic Church* teaches,

> opens to us the dimensions of his love revealed in Christ: praying with and for all who do not yet know him, so that Christ may "gather into one the children of God." God's care for all men and for the whole of creation has inspired all the great practitioners of prayer; it should extend our prayer to the full breadth of love. (2793)

That's it precisely. The prayer that Jesus taught us opens the heart to entrustment to the Father, in the constant search to carry out his will.

In his wisdom the Persian bishop Aphrahat, around the year 340, could write in his *Demonstrations*: "Look, my friend, when you are presented with a task is pleasing to the will of God, do not say: 'The time for prayer is near, I will pray and then I will do it.' While you are seeking to complete your prayer, the pleasing task that is taken from you, and you defraud God of his will and good pleasure. With your prayer you make yourself a debtor of sin. Instead, do what is pleasing to God, and that will be your prayer" (*Demonstrations* 4, 14). In other words: the prayer of the *Our Father* asks that God's will be done, but this must be sought in prayer that is turned into action. To return to the thoughts of Bishop Aphrahat: "Let man do God's will, and this will be prayer" (*Demonstrations* 4, 16). In short, prayer does not detract from the tasks of everyday life but supports them and indicates the path to follow.

+ RINO FISICHELLA

Introduction

The *Our Father* was born and took shape in the experience of the early Church, so it could be enlightening to revisit its origin and early development. That is what we propose, but let us be more specific.

We find at the beginning of the second century, the "Lord's Prayer" already in use in a formulation corresponding to the current one, in the liturgy of the early Church (cf. *Didaché*, 8, 3), where the "quadriform" Gospel also began to be read — that is, according to Mark, Matthew, Luke and John. The concurrence of the use of the Lord's Prayer and the reading of the four Gospels is significant. It constitutes the arrival point of the journey of a manifold tradition, which developed amid various events and tensions — one could simply think of the tensions within the Pauline and Johannine Churches — and culminated in the second century in what has been called "the great Church."

What is the journey that the Lord's Prayer made in the tradition that merged into the great Church? More specifically, given that the Lord's Prayer has been seen as the synthesis of the whole Gospel (Tertullian), what is its specific relationship with the "quadriform Gospel?"

An answer to this question will allow us to identify the theological-biblical structure underlying the Lord's Prayer, and to situate it in the living environment of the early Church. This will give us a framework of reference, and as a result we will see first the antecedents in Mark, then the systematic presentation of Matthew, Paul's push forward, the accentuation of Luke, and, finally, the mature synthesis found in John.

The Antecedents in Mark

Let's start with the Gospel of Mark, also called "the Gospel of the catechumen," because it is particularly suitable for Christian initiation. In it, the "twelve" make a journey of faith whose main stages coincide with the developmental stages of the Gospel text. What do we find in Mark's Gospel concerning the *Our Father*?

As is known, a liturgical formula can be found only in the Gospels of Matthew and Luke. In Mark, however, a few features can be identified that clearly prepare the way and are significant.

The disciples are gradually introduced to prayer; they are encouraged to address God with the greatest trust and confidence (cf. Mk 11:22–24). They are advised to expect everything from God as if, when they ask, they had already obtained it (v. 24). Living with Jesus, the "being with Him" typical of Mark's Gospel, gradually brings forth in the disciples their need for the Father and prepares, so to speak, the room for welcoming him.

This space is constituted first of all by the *forgiveness* that, before praying, they must grant to others: "And whenever you stand praying, forgive, if you have anything against anyone; so that your Father also who is in heaven may forgive you your trespasses" (v. 25). It is the only instance in which Mark's Gospel explicitly speaks of God as the *Father* of the disciples. This is the culmination of a journey in which, in direct contact with Jesus, they learned a deeper relationship with God and in the end understood God as Father. The fatherhood of God is never taken for granted.

Also concerning the relationship of Jesus with the Father, one can note in the Gospel of Mark a gradual manifestation. Twice there is explicit reference, but made in the third person: Jesus, speaking of the "Son of man" and indicating himself with this expression, mentions the "glory of his Father" (8:38). As for the day and time of the conclusion of history, no one knows anything "but only the Father" (13:32).

The disciples must have been particularly struck when Jesus, at the height of his interior passion in Gethsemane, asks God as a supreme gift for the fulfillment of his will, thus realizing the pinnacle of prayer for all time. At this particularly dramatic juncture, the disciples note with surprise that Jesus addresses God as Father and uses the terminology of familial tenderness: The Aramaic term "'abbah" remained imprinted upon them. This is the invocation, full of confidence and understanding, with which children address fathers within the family. And it is the only time we encounter the term in the Gospels.

Living with Jesus and hearing him speak like this,

the disciples gradually learn that God has an offer for them: In concrete terms, this is a Jesus who is always surprising and who appears to be the bearer of a kingdom that ultimately coincides with him. It is the "kingdom of God."

In contact with Jesus, the disciples are repeatedly urged to entrust their earthly concerns to him and to God. These worries are centered upon bread, a symbol of what is needed to live life. There is a section in Mark that has been dubbed *of bread* (cf. 6:30—8:29), in which the disciples, witnessing the multiplication of the loaves brought about by Jesus, are urged to delve deeper and understand: "Do you not yet perceive or understand? ... Do you not yet understand?" (8:17, 21). The object of this pressing request for understanding is total openness, entrustment to the Father who, through Jesus, gives in due time and in great abundance the bread that is needed for life. It would take time to understand that Jesus is indispensable not only for life understood in the religious sense, but simply for life as such. An understanding of Jesus is inadequate if it does not relate him to life, which appears incomplete, risky, uncertain without the nourishing presence of Jesus.

The familiarity with Jesus that the disciples gradually reach also puts them in special contact with each other. They will have to understand each other, love each other, forgive each other as Jesus is able to do with them (cf. Mk 11:25). Finally, the disciples, from the beginning of Jesus' ministry in Capernaum, are brought into contact with evil (1:23–26, 34, 39, etc.). Evil has a root that in a certain sense is transcendent, demonic, and it manifests itself in all forms of suffering that affect the integrity of physical life and mount to a presence, particularly disconcerting, of the demonic within man. Jesus harshly rebukes the unclean spirits that reveal his identity: It is up to Jesus himself to gradually declare his true reality and make it understood. The reaction to him of evil, here we could say precisely of "the evil one," is typical: Coexistence with Jesus is not possible, evil and the evil one cannot stand in his presence. The disciples learn, completely entrusting themselves to Jesus, to overcome these mysterious forces that undermine the life of man.

The observations that we are making come from passages scattered throughout the Gospel of Mark. When the disciples are imbued with all of these values, their prayer will be the spontaneous expression of them. Then they will learn to address God as Father, to desire the fulfillment of the kingdom, to entrust themselves like Jesus to his will, to trust in him in all of life's situations, to love each other, to overcome the negativity of the evil one. This gives a complete picture of the essential elements of Christian life that emerge from the Gospel of Mark. These elements dovetail neatly with the formula of the *Our Father*. We can therefore say that they prepare the way for it and assist in the understanding of its meaning and function.

The Complete Formulation of Matthew

The liturgical text of the *Our Father* takes up the formulation presented by the Gospel of Matthew (cf. 6:9–13), which we find included in the great Sermon on the Mount (chapters 5–7). An understanding of the formula requires, in the first place, attention to the context, then to the text that expresses that formula.

The context

The context of the *Our Father* is the Sermon on the Mount. And this is significant in itself. The sermon represents a relatively complete program of Christian practice, based on the initial beatitudes (cf. 5:3–11). These represent the value judgments that Jesus makes on man's fundamental choices, on the aspects of his life that are valid or not. For a good three chapters these basic choices are then developed, detailed and applied to various situations. Among the concrete situations subject to more precise application, we find typically Christian prayer. This will not have that extroverted, horizontal attitude which sometimes constituted a degeneration of prayer among the Jews — but not only them — of the time. Jesus insists that prayer is addressed to the "Father who sees in secret" (6:1, see in particular 6:5–6). Christian prayer appears as a dialogue imprinted with intense filial intimacy, which takes place between the Christian and God. Precisely because it is an intersubjective dialogue, comprehension happens on the fly. There is no need to multiply words, "as the Gentiles do" (v. 7). There was probably a tendency toward wordiness in Matthew's ecclesial community, which must also have been reflected in prayer. The Christian's relationship with the Father is instead plain, essential; it plumbs the depths.

The *Our Father* is situated within this specific context, qualified as an exquisitely Christian prayer, which starts from the heart of man and inclines to reach, so to speak, the heart of God with the essentiality, the profundity, the openness, not always definable, that characterize the mature relationship with the Father.

The *Our Father*

Let's take a closer look at how the characteristic Christian prayer is structured. An initial observation has to be made: The prayer of the *Our Father* is not taught as a fixed formula. Even if it would become such afterward in the liturgy of Matthew's community and later in that of the early Christian community, the *Our*

Father constitutes an enlivening and instructive pattern that illuminates and guides the development of prayer and life. Reducing it to a formula would mean decreasing and perhaps distorting its value. The Christian prayer inspired by the *Our Father* addresses God by calling him Father. The resonance of this term in the surroundings of Jesus and the first disciples is first of all social in nature. The father is the one who, with a sense of responsibility and concern, organizes family life and provides its members with what they need (cf. Mt 13:52). The whole family thus hinges on the father, his industriousness, his abilities, his skill, his wisdom. So, in addressing God we feel like a family, together, in the awareness that God as Father cares for us and does so adequately. In this perspective the father is also the one to whom one submits, the one whose will must be carried out.

Alongside this phenomenology, which sees the father situated in the collective setting of family, the strictly intersubjective relationship deserves to be underlined. The father, in this new perspective which is not opposed to the first but simply specifies one of its aspects, is the one who understands, the one who educates as a person, the one who understands the child and in whom the child has full confidence.

The figure of the father, understood in this twofold dimension suggested by the surroundings of Jesus and by the early Judeo-Christian community, is attributed to God. In calling God Father, therefore, the Christian feels united with him in the bond of the same family situation, and moreover feels loved and understood to the core. God is truly "your Father who sees in secret" (6:6).

Of these two aspects, the collective one is emphasized: Christians say *Our Father*, with reference to the socio-familial dimension that they are taking on. What is underlined is the fact that Christians find themselves living together, not just as a social aggregate, but by virtue of a thread that unites them, through their most intimate and personal values. The Father who "sees in secret" is also the Father who sees all things as a whole.

God thought of and felt in the categories of the father as experienced on earth remains at his transcendent level, which does not diminish his fatherhood. On the contrary: We could even say that God multiplies his divinity through his fatherhood, and his fatherhood through his divinity. Thus, we have a God who is infinitely Father and a Father who is infinitely such. All of this is indicated by the expression "who art in heaven." "Heaven" indicates God's own level, emphasizing his inaccessible reality. It is also a call to avoid any sort of trivialization: Approaching God as Father brought the risk, not so much of feeling him too near — this never happens — as of cutting him down to size, so to speak, projecting onto God the categories of the — inevitably limited — experience of earthly fatherhood. Matthew warns of this risk and puts the reader on guard against it when he contrasts the level of man with the level of the "heavenly Father," an expression typical of Matthew.

The first petition addressed to the heavenly Father concerns his name: It is asked that this be sanctified. An explanation will immediately clarify the thrust of this appeal. In the biblical cultural environment, the name stands for the person, and can never be reduced to a pure designation, to a title applied externally. The assignment, the changing of the name, indicates a change in the subject, a granting of status for the sake of a mission to be accomplished, a new capacity that is conferred. The name manifests and expresses what the person is, it is understandable only if thought of within the ambit of the person himself. In asking the Father that his name be sanctified, we are thus asking that he himself, precisely as a person, be sanctified.

At this point the problem of the meaning of "sanctification" arises. The semantic field to which the term belongs refers strictly to divinity:It indicates what is proper to and typical of God. One then wonders how any sanctification is conceivable with regard to God. The risk of a statement that goes around in circles or is even devoid of sense has suggested the alternative of interpreting sanctification in the sense of recognition. In this case we could say that "your name," that you yourself, should be recognized as holy: this is a widespread interpretation. But in the Bible the verb "sanctify" is never used to indicate a merely cognitive relationship that results in recognition. It refers to an action: used in the active form, "to sanctify" means to make holy, to make divine, to make like God; used in the passive form, it emphasizes the effect of this likening to God that is produced and realized. Then the problem returns, which appears to have no way out: how is a sanctification of the Holy, a deification of God, possible? We are given a solid basis for response in a well-known passage from the prophet Ezekiel:

> And I will *vindicate the holiness of my great name*, which has been profaned among the nations, and which you have profaned among them. And the nations will know that I am the Lord, declares the Lord God, *when through you I vindicate my holiness* before their eyes. (Ezekiel 36:23, emphasis added)

The text of Ezekiel, also considering the close contact between Matthew and the entire Old Testament, appears enlightening. The sanctification spoken of is real and is referred, in parallel, first to the name of God and then to God himself as subject. It is brought about not by means of an unthinkable addition to the holiness of God, but through an ever more widespread participation in this holiness that the people share in. According to this interpretation — already proposed by Saint Cyprian — God the Father is asked to realize and spread his holiness in his great Christian family.

The next petition concerns the kingdom of God, the kingdom of the Father who is in heaven. To understand this expression, it is necessary to hark back to the theological-biblical current of discourse regarding the kingdom that is already present in the Old Testament and then flows into the New. The "kingdom of God" is not limited to God's dominion over all creation but implies a series of initiatives pertaining to God and man, which we can summarize as follows.

First of all, there is a downward movement: in a certain sense God comes out of his inaccessibility and comes to meet man, bringing him an initiative. It is the understanding between God and man, the "covenant," as it has been explicitly called, which involves a bilateral proposal: God will act on man's behalf but asks man, in return, to observe the commandments. And it is here that an upward movement emerges: man leaves his profane level and dares to meet God in an attitude of openness and reciprocity. Acknowledging the offer that comes to him from God, man says his yes. The meeting of the two lines, downward and upward, brings about a new situation that will involve a close and familiar sharing between God and man, almost a symbiosis: this new reality is called the kingdom and is already realized in the Old Testament, at least beginning from the covenant of Sinai. As for the New Testament, on the downward line God, who has revealed himself as Father, offers man the riches of Christ, and on the upward line man, acknowledging this enhanced new offer, opens himself to it completely through the eyes of faith. The new situation thus determined is the kingdom of God in the meaning typical of the New Testament.

As has been seen there is a development, a transition from the Old Testament to the New. And in the New Testament itself there is a further impulse: The kingdom will entail an ever more permeating presence of Christ in all created reality, in men and in things, and, through Christ, an ever-closer presence on the part of God. The ultimate end of this ongoing movement will be the eschatological goal, in which, as Paul recalls, God will be "all in all" (1 Cor 15:28). The kingdom seen in this final phase belongs to the future; it is strictly eschatological.

Now let us return to our text. The Christian who asks that the kingdom of the Father "come" is joining in this forward development. What he is asking for is a greater presence of the richness of Christ among men, in their lives, in their structures, in the world they inhabit. The petition concerns both God and man, precisely because God has willed to be involved with man through the offering he makes to him.

Another petition presented to the Father concerns the realization of his will. The will of the Father is understood in the objective sense of all that God has devised for man: in the first place the commandments, all the instructions that come down to man from the word of God embodied in Christ and interpreted by the Spirit. Furthermore, given that God, the creator of all, also organizes the movement of history and does everything in view of man, we can say that a message expressing his will is also included in the history of individuals. Doing the will of God involves full docility of action with respect to this broad gamut that manifests it. It is not passive resignation but involves heartfelt sharing: the Christian becomes aware that what is best for him lies precisely in what God proposes. This brings about the desire — there is no true prayer without desire — to do his will.

This conception involves on the one hand God himself in that he loves man, has plans for him, ardently desires his full realization; on the other it involves man, who recognizes with trepidation and joy that God the Father follows him moment by moment, cares for him and manifests his will by virtue of the love he has for him.

What follows for the Christian is the ideal of adequate execution, which starting from the level of man would reach the level proper to God and bring to earth, the zone proper to man, the very totality of heaven, which is the zone of God. In this sense it is specified that the implementation of the will of God will be realized on earth, but bringing there an optimal level of transcendent perfection, something of God, a relationship with heaven.

The petition for bread is at the center of the seven petitions of Matthew's formulation. It is also what appears to be most characteristic of the Christian who addresses God as Father: it is proper for a father to give bread to his children. In effect, the petition for bread leads back to the picture of family life in which the figure of the father is situated. Bread, in the biblical cultural environment, is at the same time a concrete reality and a symbol. In realistic language, bread indicates the basic food of life. God the Father, concerning himself with the development of man's life in the concreteness of his history, as a result also takes to heart the nourishment that makes it possible. Here this consideration is reinterpreted in the perspective of the family. The nourishment that is asked of God is no longer the seed-bearing plant, as we find in Genesis 1:29, but bread, the nourishment made by man for man, which is shared within the family by the individual members. So, in addressing God specifically as Father, the Christian, precisely by appealing to the familial paternity of God, passionately asks him for the nourishment that he needs to live.

But bread is also a symbol. It evokes all that tends to make family life not only possible, but also pleasant. This means clothing, housing, in short all of those trimmings which, even if secondary to nourishment, contribute to allowing life to be lived with serenity and dignity.

Bread is requested today and for today. There is a twofold insistence on dailiness. And this is significant: it is in fact supposed that God, as Father, follows with a concern worthy of him and worthy of his children the development of their life that takes place in space and time. The Father's concern will therefore follow his children always and everywhere, without the slightest interruption. It is precisely this living, simultaneous relationship with the Father that leads his children to ask moment by moment, occasion by occasion, place by place for what is necessary and useful for their existence. They do not seek to amass treasures on earth, nor even to make provision for themselves by closing themselves off in a human calculation against the unforeseeable circumstances of the future. The Christian knows how to live day by day, because he is followed, loved, guided, and protected by the Father, without over haste or delay.

Finally, the familial framework in which the petition is situated entails the completeness of the family. The bread requested is "ours," not "mine": it is the bread of all, which reaches all. We request it for each other. The family spirit that is suggested by the biblical figure of fatherhood also entails horizontal reciprocity between Christian brothers. They must feel united as children of the Father. This awareness will then lead them to an attitude that reflects, in their reciprocity, the vertical attitude that the Father has toward them. Christians are aware that they must repay, to God the Father, their "debts." This is a symbolic image that expresses a sad reality: The emptiness, the threadbare insufficiency, that Christians too can bring about in the domain of their existence through their wrong choices, their "sins." An emptiness with respect to the context of reality/value devised by God consequently becomes a debt — according to the symbolic image used — that man contracts first and foremost with himself. But since God is Father, infinitely Father, through an appropriation of love he considers as done to himself the evil that man does to his own detriment. This process of appropriation in love takes on more precise contours in terms of, for example, covenant, commandments, laws that come from God and are an expression of his will to love. God the Father takes man seriously and wants to be taken seriously in return. If what God asks of man is not realized, a void is formed that touches God himself, a fracture is made in the relationship. God-Father follows man with an uninterrupted flow of goodness; the encounter overcomes the fractures and he fills these voids. Staying with the metaphor used, God forgives debts. He wants man to ask him for this so that he may become aware of what is at stake.

Let's see how the relationship with God the Father is realized in the concreteness of a family. The Christian has beside him other children of God who are his brothers. And since God's dealings with the individual are paradigmatic, the Christian must bring into the horizontal relationship what he receives in the vertical one. As a result, the "voids" that are opened in reciprocal relationships, the fractures, all that results in a breach of commitment that constitutes a gap, a lack of goodness, of attention, of help, of love toward each other, constitutes a list of horizontal "debts" that must be eliminated like the "debt" toward God that is to be eliminated. Otherwise, the flow of goodness that starts from God and is intended to pass through men to return to God would remain blocked.

When it comes to the horizontal level, man is in his own element: powerless to fill the voids that separate him from God, to "pay his debts" with him, the Christian can do so toward other men who are on the same level as he is. And he will have to do so. There is a demand for "family" on the part of God the Father, who wants to be imitated in this goodness, constructive to the utmost. As a result, in order to be able to invoke God as Father the Christian must first lend a hand to his brothers. God, it seems, refuses to be invoked outside of this collective family sphere and rejects anyone who presumes to come to him alone, excluding others.

Doing for others what he would desire for himself, and as for the "debts" that he has contracted, remitting, remedying, tenaciously restoring all of the deformities that are introduced into the horizontal relationship, the Christian will be sure of being welcomed by the Father.

The last two petitions of the *Our Father* in Saint Matthew also concern the mystery of sin as seen in those elements that easily influence it: *temptation* and the *evil one*. The biblical concept of temptation is unique and, rather than a concept in the strict sense, it is a cluster of concepts. Temptation takes place when certain values realized before, individually or collectively, are subjected to pressure. This pressure could be individual or collective, momentary or protracted.

The clearest example is the journey in the desert that separates the exit from Egypt and the entrance into the promised land. These are the forty years of "temptation in the desert" (cf. Ps 95:9). The values of the covenant, proposed to and accepted by the people, are subjected to multiple pressures: the everyday, the absence of dramatic events, especially the underground maturation of the group of the people of God which gradually comes together and learns to be free, and finally the pressure of uncomfortable circumstances. Temptation can have a positive outcome. This will result in a reinforcement of previous values as a fruit of the trial endured. Thus, for example, it is emphasized that Abraham was "found faithful when tested" (1 Mc 2:52; cf. Sir 27:5, 7). But given man's weakness, temptation can have a negative outcome: if the pressure of the trial exceeds man's ability to withstand it, temptation becomes the irreversible occasion of a wrong choice (cf. Mt 26:41; Mk 14:38; Lk 22:40, 46). Temptation/trial is added to the mystery of evil with which man is always in contact. This also means the mystery of his inconsistent weakness. So, God the Father is asked to intervene in his defense and keep him out of the quicksand of those temptations whose outcome would be negative.

The experience of God's people in the desert suggests another possible interpretation, in itself more in keeping with the terminology used. In Greek, "temptation" has an active meaning: rather than temptation suffered, it indicates temptation by man's initiative. In the desert the people are repeatedly led to "tempt" God, to put him to the test (cf. Ex 17:7; Dt 6:16; 9:22; Ps 95:9). This is a negative attitude because it contrasts with the trusting and unreserved abandonment that is owing to the care that God affords to his own. But it is above all a lack of filiality: it means a failure to trust and is equivalent to demanding a guarantee that would reassure man in his own sphere.

If temptation is already contact with the mystery of evil, this is enhanced when it is personified as the "evil one": It is the demonic, Satan. The experience that the Christian is able to consult both through personal observation and by listening to the Old Testament indicates to him that there is a complex network of snares, of negativity that, materializing in his history, tends to envelop him. The Christian knows that he has weak points that the demonic could seize upon, and it would be difficult for him to even be aware of this. This situation — which could lead to dramatic tension — has no impact on the underlying serenity of the children of God. God the Father has overcome the evil of history from the beginning and has destroyed it through the death of Jesus. So, he is able to adequately defend his children from it, not only by warning them but in fact by almost wresting them from the grasp of the "evil one."

This final petition constitutes, at bottom, a reminder of the reality of the Christian's precarious situation. One cannot believe, even if he is truly a child of God, that he has reached a level of safety that is above any risk. He is on the journey. So, he asks the Father to watch over his journey, to free him also from himself, from those areas within him that are subject to attack by the "evil one."

Of the seven times Jesus speaks of his "heavenly" Father, two of them have to do with Jesus himself: "my heavenly Father" (Mt 15:13; 18:35); and five with Christians: "your heavenly Father" (Mt 5:48; 6:14; 6:26, 32; 23:9).

When Christians welcome the message of Jesus and to the extent that they do so, there is as it were a transfer from Jesus to Christians.

When "my heavenly Father" has become "your heavenly Father," it is possible to say, "Our Father who art in heaven."

The *Our Father* in Saint Paul

We do not find in Paul a formulation of the *Our Father* that corresponds entirely to that of Matthew. Some elements of correspondence, however, are clearly recognizable and significant. One of them above all deserves to be studied closely: in two places Paul insists that we, as Christians led by the Spirit, turn to God and "cry, Abba, Father" (Rom 8:15; Gal 4:5–6).

It is an invocation that is situated within the liturgy, as indicated by the characteristic verb that is used, "we cry." The assembly feels the need to express out loud an invocation that directly connects it with the Father. According to some scholars, this is precisely the recitation of the *Our Father* aloud. We would thus have a close connection with the synoptic traditions, notably that of Luke. Leaving aside the *Our Father* as a formula, even an approximate one, which is still unlikely in the first years of the early phase, there is a bold impulse toward God-Father that is realized collectively: "we cry" in the liturgical assembly. Even if we do not yet have the formula, we find at least a beginning of it.

In this impulse toward the Father, it is worth noting the use of the Aramaic term "Abbà," papa, which we have come across in the Gospel of Mark, used exclusively by Jesus. According to this testimony from Paul, Christians dare to turn to God and make their own the familial intimacy, indicated precisely by Abbà, that Jesus, according to the documentation we have, had reserved for himself. The ecclesial community gradually becomes aware of the breadth of the Spirit who enlivens her, proclaims the truth of Jesus to her, formulates the law for her, and also gives her the strength to keep it. The Spirit of God and of Jesus who, "poured out" in the heart of the Christian (Rom 5:5), organizes his whole life. Since the Spirit conveys the content of Christ, an affinity is produced with Christ himself, which, entering little by little into the life of the Christian, also penetrates his consciousness. In the sphere of the new awareness that this brings about, the Spirit bears witness to the Christian of his reality, his filiation (cf. Rom 8:16). This makes it understandable how the community could dare to address the Father with the same familiarity as that of Christ.

If this is the aspect closest to the *Our Father* that we find in the Pauline sphere, there is no lack of other points of contact of some interest. We will limit ourselves to a few examples. Paul shows a particular sensibility for the fatherhood of God. God is normally called "Our Father and the Lord Jesus Christ" (Rom 1:7; 1 Cor 1:3; 2 Cor 1:2, 3; Gal 1:3, etc.). Paul regularly makes a pairing between the fatherhood of God with regard to us and the fatherhood of God with regard to Jesus Christ. Our filiation is not only placed alongside that of the Son but depends on the "first-born among many brothers and sisters" (Rom 8:29). In relationship with Christ, being in contact with him, the Christian perceives that he has an open path, even a push toward the Father (cf. Rom 5:1; 1 Cor 8:6). He constantly moves at the level of "Abbà-Father." It is noteworthy that Paul never uses the term "heavenly" to refer to God the Father, nor does he explicitly relate him with "heaven."

The participation of the Christian community in God's holiness occurs, for the apostle, through the decisive influence of the Spirit, explicitly called "the Spirit of holiness" (Rom 1:4). This begins with baptism, on the basis of which Christians are called "saints" and "sanctified."

Precisely because it stems from baptism, the holiness of the Christian is entirely related to Christ. One of the densest statements on this matter is found in 1 Corinthians 1:30: "[God] is the source of your life in Christ Jesus, whom God made our wisdom, our righteousness and sanctification and redemption." It is clear that the sanctification that Christ brings to us, coming "from God," is nothing but a participation in the holiness of God, a participation that is realized and spreads in the realm of the community's "we."

The kingdom of God in Paul, unlike in the synoptic

Gospels, is in the future, with an eschatological significance. Consequently, the kingdom about which the petition "come" is made will be constituted by the participation of all and of everything in the resurrection of Christ, as will be realized when the Son "delivers the kingdom to God the Father" (1 Cor 15:24) and God will be "all in all" (1 Cor 15:28).

Thy will be done

Paul develops the theme of God's will in a particular way. On the one hand there is, always present and in the foreground, "God who wills." One understands the will of God if before looking at the objective content that it expresses one establishes a lively contact with God as Father: his is "the will of our God and *Father*" (Gal 1:4, emphasis added), as he reveals himself over the span of salvation history from the Old to the New Testament. The will of God passes through personal involvement, and in parallel with his "good pleasure" (cf. Eph 1:9). The other "pole" of God's will in Paul is its objective content. In summary, we could say that God's will as objective content is entirely distilled in Christ. We find God's will expressed in Christ, in his teaching, in his behavior, in his person. The Spirit will take this "raw material" concentrated in Christ and will take care to "proclaim" it to the Christian moment by moment, situation by situation.

Give us this day our bread

Paul does not insist on the request for bread. But various references show that this aspect is also present to him.

Of the ten references to "bread," seven concern the Eucharistic bread and three refer to bread in the usual sense, with the accent on the effort of work (2 Thess 3:8, 12), and, above all, on trust in God who "supplies seed to the sower and bread for food" (2 Cor 9:10). We are within the circuit of the filial request for bread that we found in Matthew. Above all, Paul is concerned with placing nourishment within the grand context of the liturgy of life, on the basis of which everything is referred to God: "So, whether you eat or drink, or whatever you do, do all to the glory of God" (1 Cor 10:31).

Deliver us from evil

As for the overcoming of evil expressed by Matthew with the metaphor of the remission of debt, Paul digs deep. He shows that he has fully grasped the meaning of the Sermon on the Mount (cf. Mt 5:38–48) and reworks it with those capacities of concentration and essentiality that are characteristic of him. With a direct reference to the Sermon on the Mount, the apostle states that when faced with those who harm him the Christian must have a constructive attitude, even to the point of giving food and drink to his enemy (Rom 12:20). "Do not be overcome by evil," Paul says to the

Christian, "but overcome evil with good" (Rom 12:21).

That's already quite a bit, but Paul is not satisfied. Developing the metaphor of debt in an original way and in a positive perspective, he decisively affirms that the Christian is always and only a debtor of love: "Owe no one anything, except to love each other" (Rom 13:8). The development with respect to the level indicated by Matthew is truly remarkable. It is no longer a matter of getting past the points of hostility that come from others, simply letting them drop, not considering them, remitting "the debt." One goes on the counterattack. If the only debt truly is love, this will be the attitude to which the Christian will feel obliged toward his brothers and, more generally, toward all men.

No form of evil will find him unprepared, in a situation of dreamy naivety, nor simply willing to systematically ignore the harm done to him. The Christian will have a constructive attitude. He will not let evil defeat him, not only in the sense of not using the same weapons, but above all in the sense of not being coerced by its pessimism. Evil can and will be overcome, but only through a flood of goodness.

Do not abandon us to temptations

As for temptation, we find in Paul a complex and elaborate case study. Paul had personal and painful experience of trial; he felt "harassed" by Satan (cf. 2 Cor 12:7–10). He therefore speaks of it with that personal involvement which is a typical attitude of his: what he experiences personally, Paul presents as paradigmatic for others. He insists on two aspects that he considers fundamental: temptation/trial must be accepted by the Christian, who will also have to equip himself adequately to defend himself. This is a real battle, which must therefore be faced as such (Eph 6:10–17). God allows it so that the Christian may grow stronger, and watches over him that he not be tempted beyond his ability to resist 1 Cor 10:13).

But good will, even translated into a realistic commitment to defense, is not enough: recourse to God in prayer is needed to prevent temptations from unfolding according to the insidious intentions of the tempter, Satan (cf. 2 Cor 2:11; 11:14; 2 Thes 2:9). In temptation the mystery of evil and the evil one converge with the unknowns of the human heart, with its ability of endurance and its unforeseen surrenders. There is the need for the strength of God and Christ so that the Christian may "get out" of temptation without remaining a prisoner (1 Cor 10:13).

A parallel discussion can be held regarding the "evil one." Paul notes his presence in history, with an arrogant and insidious power. Satan can insinuate himself into all aspects of concrete life; he can wait for the Christian at any turning point in his journey and act, becoming temptation. The Christian, however, must not live under the nightmare of the demonic. The seriousness of what is at stake remains, but it is adherence to Christ, fueled by prayer, which will allow him to overcome the demonic and to live his filiation with joy.

In summary: the elements of the *Our Father* can also be seen in Paul. They are found in a fluid state, which we could however say is incandescent. The unequivocally liturgical dimension in which the invocation "Abbà-Father" is situated brings us back, if not necessarily to the formula of the *Our Father*, then to an equivalent fragment of prayer, notable for its intensity and for the pervasive influence of the Spirit. But the "fluid state" is determined by the manifold experience of life in which the elements corresponding to the formula appear incorporated. There is, we could say, a kind of pendular movement: from the liturgical formulation to Christian life, from Christian life to the formulation. This sets off a mechanism of going ever deeper, which also leads to essentiality. That is what we find in Luke's presentation.

The *Our Father* in Luke

As we observed at the beginning, we also find a formula of the *Our Father* in Luke. It is worth taking a closer look at this. To understand it we must keep a general fact in mind: the close contact between Luke and Paul, which can be seen in the Book of Acts written by Luke and which also leaves its mark on the Gospel. What we have observed in Paul, we therefore expect to find in Luke as well. This brings us to the formula of the *Our Father*.

While Matthew sets this within the Sermon on the Mount, in the context of a prayer that is supposed to avoid pagan wordiness, Luke gives a few more concrete references related to the attitude of Jesus. Jesus prays. To do so, he often retreats to solitary places, even isolating himself from the disciples. They become aware of this, admire the Master's behavior and are prompted to imitate him. So, they ask him, "Lord, teach us to pray" (Lk 11:1). Jesus' response is compelling. He says to them, "When you pray, say" (Lk 11:2). The disciples are presumed to have a volition to pray that is determined, serious, committed. The formula that Jesus suggests is therefore the perceptible expression of a prayer that first moves from the inside. Then comes Luke's typical formulation. The prayer is addressed to the "Father." Matthew's clarification "who art in heaven" is not added. It has been asked why this should be. Discarding the fanciful hypothesis that Jesus taught two formulas, it has been thought with good reason that this apparent simplification by Luke in reality constitutes a deeper focus. This is what W. Marchel maintains. And the deeper focus would be this: "Father" closely recalls the Aramaic term "Abbà," and constitutes its most immediate and spontaneous translation. So, it could be said that we find in Luke what in Paul appeared as a cry to the Father, expressed with the familial intimacy that Jesus used in his earthly life and that the Spirit elicits in Christians.

We would therefore have Paul's foundation elaborated in a formula. This solid foundation of a prayer that is known and felt to be animated by the Spirit of Jesus and therefore leads to addressing God simply by calling him Father makes it superfluous to add "who art in heaven," in the sense that this has already been established. Let's clarify. Not even in Matthew is this a matter of a warning, almost as if the disciples were being told not to forget, when they invoke God as Father, that he is in heaven and not immediately available on earth. The meaning is deeper because it involves the transcendence of God. It is precisely the action of the Spirit that in a certain way brings transcendence into direct contact with man. If it is truly the Spirit who enlivens the prayer of the Christian and drives him to turn to the Father, there is an impulse toward transcendence that unfolds within man. It can be stated without exaggeration that "heaven" is found in the heart of man, in the sense that it is precisely in the heart that the Spirit acts, who has been "poured out" there (Rom 5:5).

The sanctification of God's name and the coming of his kingdom take on particular clarity. Here too the sanctification of the name is the spread of God's personal holiness within the Christian community. The kingdom whose near presence is desired is the one glimpsed in Matthew, perhaps with an accentuation of its movement toward the eschatological conclusion. As a result, the coming of the kingdom always refers to that reality which is born when the descending and ascending lines meet. The word-for-word concurrence of these two petitions, as well as the change in the basic invocation, suggests a common contact of the tradition of Luke and of Matthew with the Q source, which however results in an original elaboration by Luke that appears first of all in the omissions. For example, we do not find the petition, as is explicitly highlighted in Matthew, of the fulfillment of God's will. Here too, rather than an absence, it is a matter of a deeper focus. We have seen in Paul, who is likely the model for Luke, how the will of God epitomized in Christ is conveyed and proposed concretely to man by the action of the Spirit. Then the problem shifts. God is not asked that his will be carried out with a perfection that implies transcendence, because all of this is already underway: the illumination and impulse of the Spirit leads to the moment-by-moment identification and fulfillment of the will of God. Consequently, the actual problem for the Christian is docility to the Spirit. The will of the Father is thus realized in the here and now, with an organic quality that penetrates all aspects of life, without gaps and without interruption.

A few characteristics of Luke

We find, instead, a particular insistence in the petition for bread: Luke emphasizes the everyday. While Matthew insists on the bread that is requested "this day" (Mt 6:11), Luke clarifies by adding "give us each day our daily bread." This is a significant nuance. It is asked that God grant bread according to the plan that he himself has established, concerning the continuity of life that unfolds day by day. It is clear that the bread that is needed today is asked for now, with that attitude of simultaneity with regard to the Father which we have already noted. But it is likewise clear, and this is the meaning of the nuance in Luke, that what is requested is not an infinite supply, nor even a supply that would last more than a day. Just as the manna was given by God in the desert day by day (cf. Ex 16:1–20; Wis 16:20–21), so also bread is requested with its own daily rhythm according to God's plan. In this way, on the one hand we ask with insistence, while on the other we entrust ourselves fully to God.

The next petition is "forgive us our sins, for we ourselves forgive everyone who is indebted to us" (Lk 11:4). In comparison with Matthew's formulation, this one presents a twofold variation that ought to be clarified. What in Matthew are called "debts" are here called "sins." This is an interpretation that tends to broaden the meaning of the metaphor "debts," as if Luke wanted to tell us not to think only of those "debts" contracted with God by way of formal breaches, which in the practice of the Old Testament could be overcome through a well-defined ritual offering in proportion to the extent of the transgression. Debts are sins — that is, every time man does wrong, going outside of the proper context devised for him by God, the result is sin. Sin always concerns God, not only when the wrongful action is aimed directly at him — as in blasphemy — but also when the sinful decision affects man alone. God loves man as Father and does not tolerate, given the irresistible strength of his love, that his child should be hurt. But when the sinful decision has been made and the evil has been brought about, only God can remedy it, through that new creation which is his way of forgiving. In asking the Father to forgive our sins, we are asking him for a total restoration, even a creative action regarding that void, that "nothingness," which has been produced in our system through sin.

The restorative reparation with respect to the void of sin is asked of God in direct proportion with a constructive attitude toward others. Luke replaces the term "debts" with the term "sins" in regard to God but leaves the metaphor of "debts" to be remitted when it comes to the Christian's attitude toward his brothers. This too is significant. The chasm opened by sin is wider than the "debts" that are contracted with each other in everyday life. Their remission involves the constant need to re-establish a balance disturbed, not to rebuild a void.

A final nuance brought to the fore regarding the continued forgiveness of "debts" that others contract toward us is its universality. Obviously in Matthew as well any exception to this provision of remission would be inadmissible. But Luke makes it explicit. We ask for the remission of our sins, adding "for we ourselves forgive everyone who is indebted to us" (Lk 11:4). It comes across like a challenge: there could always be brothers or men in general who will have a negative impact on the Christian, injuring his rights and becoming "debtors." Faced with any action of this kind, above all when faced with any person who behaves like this, the Christian will always have just one response: to forgive the debt with the joy of imitating the goodness of the Father — *"for we ourselves"* — and the goodness of Jesus, who on the cross said, "Father, forgive them ..." (Lk 23:34).

Finally, in Luke we find a simplification of the last petition regarding temptation and the evil one. The "deliver us from the evil one" part is dropped, leaving only the petition "lead us not into temptation." In all likelihood the reason for this omission lies in the direction of a focus that also tends to simplify the discourse. We have seen how the demonic, in Paul's rethinking of it, does not act alone but infiltrates human structures, putting pressure on man through them. Pressure toward the wrongful choice of sin is temptation, which does not remain isolated: if there is temptation there is also a tempter who activates it. Keeping this fact in mind, liberation from the evil one is already contained in the request not to get caught up in temptation. In other words: temptation will happen, but as long as one gets through it, it can even have a positive purpose. But it will take special support from God, to be obtained with prayer, to keep the inevitable temptation from turning into a deadly trap. Overcoming temptation involves neutralizing the effect of the demonic, and therefore a full liberation from its negative influence. A temptation that comes from man alone could hardly have an impact so strong and worrying as to require turning to the Father to escape unscathed.

The *Our Father* in John

The Johannine movement represents a particularly advanced ecclesiastical experience within the domain of the New Testament. We can situate it, as to its most mature expression, between the years 80–120 in the region of Ephesus. Typical representatives are certainly the fourth Gospel and the letters of John, and probably also Revelation. So, the question arises as to whether, and in what way, the Lord's Prayer may be reflected as a formulation or above all as content in this stratum of the early Church.

An initial approach threatens disappointment: a formula of prayer that directly suggests that the *Our Father* does not appear documented in the field of the Johannine writings. These undoubtedly speak of prayer, insist on prayer to be addressed to the Father in the name of Jesus (cf. Jn 15:16; 16:23–24), and emphasize prayer that is addressed to Jesus himself and asks in his name, but prayer addressed directly by Christians to the Father and identifiable in any formula or schematization, that we do not find.

Jesus prays to the Father

Instead, we find a prayer addressed precisely to the Father and expressed directly by Jesus: it is chapter 17 of the fourth Gospel. Is there a certain relationship between this prayer, highlighted emphatically by the evangelist, and the Lord's Prayer that is presented to us in the Synoptics and to which Paul probably makes that fragmentary allusion which we have examined? Answering this question requires careful contextualization. We must clarify the relationship between Jesus and the Father that stands out in such a special way in this prayer but begins earlier and is documented throughout the fourth Gospel.

In the Gospel, Jesus is presented from the beginning as "full of grace and truth … as of the only Son from the Father" (Jn 1:14). As the only-begotten Son, he has a complete relationship with the Father, and the fourth Gospel takes care to make this explicit. A few reminders should suffice, given that it is a well-known aspect.

The whole life of Jesus is regulated by the Father. It unfolds, we could say, in the light of the Father, moment by moment, hour by hour (cf. Jn 11:9–10) in a continuous dialogic situation. And this means that Jesus is always in action, just as the Father is in action (5:17). What the Father does is paradigmatic for Jesus in the most absolute way: it is enough that the Father do something for Jesus to want and almost need to do it too. There is between Jesus and the Father a perfect operational harmony (5:19). But this is not a matter of mechanical parallelism. This perfect reciprocity is the fruit of a dizzying love that exists between the two, which Jesus recognizes and expresses almost with amazement, and certainly with joy: "For the Father loves the Son and shows him all that he himself is doing" (5:20). And love moves the Father to show the Son what he does and what the Son will accept as the Father's will (5:30).

The Son shows an enthusiastic passion for the will of the Father, which constitutes "[his] food" (cf. Jn 4:34); his ideal is to "always do the things that are pleasing to him" (8:29). This utmost reciprocity leads Jesus to the gift of himself.

When the "hour" approaches — of death and resurrection — Jesus feels a shudder: it is the human reaction in the face of suffering and death (cf. Jn 12:27). After asking the Father to free him from the "hour," he collects himself immediately and reiterates to himself that he has come into the world precisely to live that "hour," and expresses to the Father what is the most ardent desire he feels: "Father, glorify your name" (v. 28). The answer that comes from the Father has already been realized in the concrete existence of Jesus before the "hour," and will find its culminating expression in the "hour" itself: "And I, when I am lifted up from the earth, will draw all people to myself" (v. 32). This is an unequivocal reference to death on the cross, which represents the pinnacle of the work of Jesus and his relationship with the Father.

Beginning the "hour" with his passion, Jesus would solemnly declare to his disciples: "I do as the Father has commanded me, so that the world may know that I love the Father" (14:31). This relationship of maximum mutual openness with the implications we have seen between Jesus and the Father gives the finishing touch to the "prayer of the hour" with which we started and which we could call the *Our Father* of Jesus. Jesus turns to the Father, raising "his eyes to heaven" (17:1). But transcendence, evoked by the term "heaven," is within himself: "I am in the Father and the Father in me" (14:10). They are "one" (10:30). The prayer of the "hour" unfolds in three concentric circles. In the first, Jesus speaks to the Father about himself; he asks for his glorification in order to be able to glorify the Father in turn, thus giving to men what the Father has given to him: eternal life (cf. Jn 17:1–5). In the second concentric circle Jesus speaks to the Father about his disciples (17:6–19): they have received the manifestation of the "man" of the Father. Jesus asks the Father to always take care of them in relation to "your name, which you have given me" (v. 11), so that they, sharing the reality of the Father and of Jesus, "may be one, even as we are one" (v. 11). This stupendous situation will have to be defended, and Jesus prays to the Father to keep them "from the evil one" (v.15). In the third circle (17:20–25) Jesus' prayer to the Father extends to all those who believe in him. Jesus gives them his "glory" (v. 22), his reality/value. As a result, they will all be, no less than the disciples, "one, just as you, Father, are in me, and I in you" (v. 21). And all of this is pushed to an eschatological level, according to the category of John's own realized eschatology: "Father, I desire that they also, whom you have given me, may be with me where I am, to see my glory that you have given me because you loved me before the foundation of the world" (v. 24).

An almighty *Our Father*

The points of contact between the prayer of the hour and the *Our Father* are numerous and evocative. The invocation of God as Father, put in the mouth of Jesus, takes up and surpasses the intimacy with the Father as found in Luke. The reference to heaven is reinterpreted. There is repeated mention of the "name" of the Father, meaning his person. The holiness that is realized in sharing by the Christian community in John 17 is glory, in the aforementioned sense of reality/value that passes from the Father to Jesus and from Jesus to his own, starting with the disciples, with the final result of a transcendent unity between the Father, Jesus, and them which is thus achieved.

The ecclesial community seen in this perspective as "one," both reciprocally and with respect to the Father and to Jesus, constitutes a particularly stimulating interpretation of the kingdom, in the sense indicated above: it is the situation that is determined by the encounter of the descending line whereby the Father so loves the world that he offers and gives the Son (cf. Jn 3:16) with the ascending line constituted by man's acceptance of faith. If the disciples and Christians will then truly be one vertically and horizontally, they will fully carry out the will of the Father and will love each other to the fullest. Their presence in the world will expose them to temptations. Jesus does not want them to be snatched away but prays to the Father to "keep them from the evil one," as we find in the Matthean formulation. To sum up: the absence of the *Our Father* is only apparent.

In reality we find in the prayer of the hour an enhanced reformulation of what constitutes its underlying petitions: we have the *Our Father* of Jesus.

John teaches in the first place that the disciples pray by learning from Jesus. So, is it possible to identify, following the contours of the *Our Father*, the points of interest on which the prayer of the Johannine community must have been particularly insistent? How did the Johannine Church learn to pray, in continuity with the first disciples?

We start from a consideration that at first glance seems obvious: the prayer of Jesus with which the Christian addresses the Father assumes that he is the Son of God. In the Johannine movement, filiation with regard to God is deeply felt: it affirms from the beginning the "power" given to those who believe in Jesus "to become children of God" (Jn 1:12). Those who, having believed, have this power certainly include the disciples. But although as the fourth Gospel unfolds it speaks very often of the relationship of filiation between the Father and Jesus, it does not emphasize the filiation of the disciples. This is only spoken of as an event that occurrs in the context of the "hour" when the risen Jesus, speaking of them, explicitly characterizes them as his "brethren" and says "I am ascending to my Father and your Father, to my God and your God" (Jn 20:17). The power to become children of God at this point appears realized. It constituted a journey that took place within the "book of signs" (Jn 1:19—12:50): the disciples, being in direct contact with Jesus, gradually expanded and strengthened their capacity to accept it. They imbued themselves with his word and his truth, expressing their appreciation for this even in times of crisis (cf. for example the profession of Peter, "You have the words of eternal life," after the Eucharistic discourse, cf. 6:68).

Matured in this progressive acceptance of Jesus, the disciples in the book of the "hour" make a qualitative leap precisely in their filiation: Jesus, whom they have admired for his reality, his value and his "glory" ("we have seen his glory, glory as of the only Son from the Father," Jn 1:14), communicates to them this characterization of his. He states this in the prayer of the hour that we have already seen: "The glory which you have given me I have given to them, that they may be one even as we are one" (17:22). It is participation in the "glory," in the reality/value proper to the Son, that actualizes in the disciples and in all those who believe through their word the "power" to become children of God, in a relationship of the closest union with Jesus, with the Father (cf. 17:23) and with each other.

This lofty realization of filiation brings joy (cf. 17:13), peace, and sanctification (v. 19), all directly related to the influence of Jesus, to the participation that he gives in himself.

And the most characteristic consequence is prayer. Jesus, starting with the "book of signs," practices a continuous dialogic prayer toward the Father, which every now and then becomes explicit in its content (cf. Jn 6:11: "when he had given thanks"; and especially 11:41). And yet there is never any mention of a prayer addressed to the Father by the disciples. But now that by participating in the "glory" of Jesus they too have become children, they are expressly encouraged by Jesus to pray in his name: "Whatever you ask of the Father in my name, he will give it to you. *Until now you have asked nothing in my name*. Ask and you will receive, that your joy may be full" (16:23–24, emphasis added).

We can say, in conclusion, that once the disciples have gradually reached the full level of their filiation, they are able to express, in perfect harmony with Jesus, their prayer to the Father. Jesus involves them in his relationship with the Father. Consequently, the prayer of the disciples and of all Christians will always be a prayer carried out at the level of Jesus, in harmony with whom the disciples turn to the Father and will tend to take on and elaborate the typical features of his truth.

The first Christian community

Following the outline of the *Our Father*, a few clarifications can be advanced. We can make these legitimately because it is highly probable that at the end of the first century, in the Johannine Church centered around Ephesus, the Matthean-Lucan formula of the *Our Father* was already known and being used in the liturgy. This likelihood is suggested by the close relationship of Paul and Luke with Ephesus; Matthew too, explicitly mentioned by Papias of Hierapolis, who was in the region of Ephesus a few decades later, must have been read and known. The "quadriform Gospel" was taking shape.

The disciples, and more generally the Christians of the Johannine school, as we find them in the first letter, would be concerned with glorifying the name of the Father as Jesus had been. We find precisely this aspect made explicit, corresponding to the first petition of the *Our Father*. The disciples hear Jesus say to them, "Whatever you ask in my name, this I will do, that the Father may be glorified in the Son" (Jn 14:13). The glorification/sanctification of the Father, in the sense of participation by the ecclesial community as indicated above, is realized as a result of the prayer of the disciples.

As we have already seen, the glorification/sanctification of the glory of the Father is realized "in the Son" and, in particular, in the "exaltation" of Jesus. It is his situation as crucified, seen as a kingship universal in its scope (cf. 19:19–22), as an indivisible unity (19:23–24), in a new relationship that is established between Mary and the new brothers of Jesus (19:25–27). This becomes visible starting from the death of Jesus, which portrays how the last pang of love toward the Father and toward men leads Jesus to his supreme perfection (19:28–30), and finally to that profusion of gifts including the Spirit which brings about the sacramental nature of the Church symbolized by the water and blood that come out of Jesus' open side, which is particularly evocative (19:31–37). This context of sanctification/glorification shows the Christian the vast horizon in which he moves when he asks the Father, using Matthew's formula, probably already widespread also in the Johannine communities, "hallowed be thy name."

Thinking of the kingdom of God, the disciples see this connected to Jesus: "Rabbi, you are the Son of God! You are the King of Israel!" (1:49). Realizing in the crucifixion (cf. 19:19–22) his "kingdom … not of this world" (18:36), Jesus makes Christians a "kingdom" (Rv 1:6), engaging them, through the exercise of their priestly mediation, in the realization of the "kingdom of the world" as "the kingdom of our Lord and of his Christ." Therefore the Christian who asks the Father for the coming of the Kingdom is in fact asking for a particular presence of Jesus with the potentiality of his situation as crucified, with the ability to draw everything and everyone to himself, first within the Christian community and then in the whole world.

Seeing how Jesus passionately loves and carries out the will of the Father, the Johannine Church grasps what it means to ask to do the will of the Father "on earth as it is in heaven": the will of the Father carried out by Jesus expresses on the earthly level the transcendence — "as it is in heaven" — of the execution of the Father's will; that will which the Christian finds in the truth of Jesus, performed under the continuous influence of the Spirit who interprets it for him (cf. Jn 16:13). The petition to do the will of the Father will therefore be in full harmony with the attitude of Jesus in this regard and oriented, concretely, toward "doing" the truth (cf. 3:21; 1 Jn 1:6).

The petition to the Father for daily bread takes on particular importance in John. The whole of chapter 6 is dedicated to an exploration of what bread represents for Christians. In it we find that Jesus, putting his divinity at the service of man, gives him food (cf. Jn 6:1–13). In the synagogue of Capernaum the following day, he himself explains the scope of this "sign," which provides a glimpse of the different levels according to which Jesus realizes himself as bread. Bread in the realistic sense, eaten the day before together with fish, is in continuity with bread in the symbolic sense. The group is urged to understand this to the full: Jesus is the "living bread which came down from heaven" (6:51), and was given by the Father (6:32). The nourishment that must be asked of the Father is therefore Jesus himself, "the bread of life" (6:48), with the versatility of nourishment that this entails: He nourishes with his word, with his example, with the Spirit; nourishes in particular with the Eucharist (6:52–59), which is insisted upon to the point of causing a distress in the listeners that can be overcome only with the dizzying faith requested by Jesus (6:60–69). Thus, one glimpses the outcome of those implications contained in the request for bread which the texts of both Matthew and Luke suggest.

In short, in John's reworking the Father gives Jesus as bread and Jesus carries out this function both by concerning himself with the needs of a physical existence to be led on this earth and by giving himself fully. Thus Jesus is understood and felt by the Church of John as the one who is able to fully nourish that life as children which allows Christians to create a particularly close relationship, anxious and joyful at the same time, with the heavenly Father: "See what kind of love the Father has given to us, that we should be called children of God; and so we are" (1 Jn 3:1).

The petition for forgiveness is reinterpreted and explored. Forgiveness comes through Jesus, through whom the Christian passes from death to life and is completely liberated from sin. This passage sets the tone for all ecclesial life: the Christian, for one thing, as a child of God who abides in him, "does not sin" (cf. 1 Jn 3:6). And beyond the risk of that essentially negative choice, sin is understood as a rejection of the law of the Spirit who now guides him (1 Jn 3:4). There may, however, be partial insufficiencies, risks, fears: the recourse to Jesus who permanently maintains his function as liberator from sin (1 Jn 2:1), an unconditional trust in a God "greater than our heart" (1 Jn 3:20), will allow Christians to live appropriately in the situation of children of God — children of God and brothers among themselves. John insists a great deal on this dimension. He does not explicitly speak of the forgiveness of offenses, but clearly incorporates this into a broader and more engaging vision.

Brotherly love, practiced appropriately, constitutes a diagnostic criterion in overcoming the situation of death proper to sin: "We know that we have passed out of death into life, because we love the brothers and sisters. Whoever does not love abides in death" (1 Jn 3:14). In positive terms, the filial relationship that is established with God, who in John's vocabulary is always the Father, is love, and is immediately poured out upon the brothers: "Beloved, let us love one another, for love is from God, and whoever loves has been born of God and knows God. Anyone who does not love does not know God, because God is love" (1 Jn

4:7–8). While Matthew and Luke emphasize an imitation of the Father in the remission of "debts" and of "sins," John boldly extends the emulation of the Father in a constructive and unlimited perspective. There is already a commitment made to love as he loves who is love, with the same intensity, with the same style: "Beloved, if God [the Father] so loved us, we also ought to love one another" (1 Jn 4:11). The realization of this kind of love in the Church will make the features of the Father recognizable (cf. v. 12).

As for the last petition of the *Our Father*, the defense from temptation and from the evil one, we once again have a Christological emphasis. Jesus explicitly asks the Father to defend the disciples from evil or the "evil one" (Jn 17:15). Having overcome the world (cf. 16:33), being superior to the "prince of this world" (16:32), he is able to guarantee for the Christian the overcoming of all demonic snares. Such snares will make themselves felt: this is highlighted in a particular way by the book of Revelation, which shows how the demonic acts by infiltrating the structures of history. Christians will always be able to conquer because they are partakers in the "blood of the lamb" (Rv 12:11) — that is, of the vitality symbolized by blood that Christ as "lamb" (cf. Rv 5:6) has obtained for his own and continually gives, drawing on the resources of his death and resurrection.

As can be seen at the end of this brief investigation, we certainly find in John an ephemeral optimism that disregards evil. Indeed, it comes as a surprise to see the accentuation, typical of the fourth Gospel, of the power of darkness (cf. Jn 1:5; 8:12; 12:35; etc.). The Christian, nonetheless, united with Christ and "abiding in" him, feels above this. His prayer can and must be addressed to the Father in part so as to overcome the snares of evil, but his main concern will be that of maintaining contact with Christ, of being and remaining a branch united with the vine (Jn 15:2); in short, to always be pervaded by the vitality of Christ. In this situation the Christian will be able to overcome evil in all its forms, even the most threatening.

We find in John a development suggestive of the underlying core expressed and detailed in the *Our Father*. No aspect is absent. But along with this presence identifiable in the details, there emerges in John the synthesis that the Christian community has developed and continues to develop, journeying onward, maturing, realizing ever more and ever better the great values of which it is the bearer. And the values that the Christian community realizes have just one name: Christ. It is Christ, with his truth and his life, who is continually given to the community through the mediation of the Spirit. And so the Father sanctifies and glorifies his name, ushers man into a kingdom that is realized day by day, establishes a reciprocity of love that leads to a passionate desire for the fulfillment of his will. In giving Christ as nourishment, the Father gives what is best for man, for his present and future life, driving him to love with his own kind of love and defending him from any snare. Moving in the orbit of Christ, the Christian will become fully a child of the Father.

Conclusion

This brief examination conducted on the main texts of the New Testament that concern it, the ramifications of which are even more extensive if one thinks, for example, of the conception of the will of the Father in the Letter to the Hebrews, presents us with an *Our Father* in movement. It begins with Mark, where the constituent elements are not yet connected to each other in a formula of prayer. Next comes the formula that is presented in Matthew and Luke, but the values that it expresses, far from being separable from the context of the respective Gospels, find themselves reinterpreted and deepened there. Paul, emphasizing the law of the Spirit, delves deep: he makes the community reflect on the significance of the fatherhood of God and the implications it entails. John, finally, offers a mature and entirely Christ-centered reworking of the core components of the *Our Father*.

So we see — this is a self-evident conclusion — that the formula of the *Our Father* is not stereotyped, but becomes like the tip of an iceberg: it makes its way through the Church, raising echoes wide and deep; it encourages the Church to mature and at the same time manages to condense and re-express the maturation that has taken place.

The pattern of development that we have noted from the Jesus of Mark to the formula of Matthew and Luke, and from the formula to the Jesus active in the Church through the Spirit that is characteristic of John, corresponds to what we find condensed in the introductory formula of the *Catechism of the Catholic Church*, illuminated in depth. As "the summary of the whole Gospel," the *Our Father* is condensed in Jesus, who is "at the center of the Scriptures"; it is made explicit in the formula of the "Lord's Prayer" and becomes the "prayer of the Church" (cf. 2759–2772).

The *Our Father* is a formula. The Church has favored the form of Matthew, which is the most fully developed and has established itself in liturgical use. This formula is analyzed and summarized in its seven petitions: it is constantly referred to. In the prayer of the Church all seven petitions are essential, even though all of them need not be presented at the same time. This formula is a distillation of life. It sees the confluence of those values which the experience of the Church has matured and developed in her history, similarly to what we find in the Pauline communities and in those underlying the Gospels.

It is essential to recall one fundamental fact: The *Our Father* continues to make its way in the contemporary Church, just as it developed in the early one.

The very numerous commentaries that have been produced throughout the span of Church history duly reflect the issues of the various historical situations, summarizing and interpreting them. All of these follow one stage of this long journey of the *Our Father* in the life of the Church. A stage that will not be the last. The Lord's Prayer will continue its function of synthesis and inspiration, like the heartbeat of the Gospel until the end of the ages.

In preparation for the Jubilee Year 2025, the Exploring Prayer series delves into the various dimensions of prayer in the Christian life. These brief, accessible books can help you learn to dialogue with God and rediscover the beauty of trusting in the Lord with humility and joy.

Prayer Today: A Challenge to Overcome
Notes on Prayer: Volume 1
by Angelo Comastri
In order to have saints, what is needed are people of authentic prayer, and authentic prayer is that which inflames with a fire of love. Only in this way is it possible to lift the world and bring it near to the heart of God. To pray in truth, we must present ourselves before God with the open wounds of our smallness and our sin. Only in this way will the encounter with God be an encounter of liberation and redemption.

Praying with the Psalms
Notes on Prayer: Volume 2
by Gianfranco Ravasi
This little guide to the Psalms includes four cardinal points: a general reflection on prayer, the breath of the soul; a panoramic look at the psalmic texts; a portrait of the two protagonists, God and the worshipper, but also the intrusion of the presence of evil; and finally, an anthology of brief commentaries on the Psalms most dear to tradition and the liturgy. The hope is that all the faithful may draw fully from this wonderful treasury of prayers.

The Jesus Prayer
Notes on Prayer: Volume 3
by Juan Lopez Vergara
This book explores the unique experience of the fatherhood of God for Jesus Christ, whom he calls Abba — which in his native Aramaic language means "Dad." Throughout his earthly life, Jesus is in contact dialogue with Abba. From his Baptism in the Jordan through his public ministry and ultimately his crucifixion, this relationship will mark him forever, transforming his life, and our lives, too.

Praying with Saints and Sinners
Notes on Prayer: Volume 4
by Paul Brendan Murray
The saints whose writings on prayer and meditation

are explored in this book are among the most celebrated in the great spiritual tradition. The aim of this book is to discover what help the great saints can offer those of us who desire to make progress in the life of prayer, but who find ourselves being constantly deflected from our purpose, our tentative efforts undermined perhaps most of all by human weakness.

Parables on Prayer
Notes on Prayer: Volume 5
by Anthony Pitta
What characterizes, in a singular way, Jesus's teaching on prayer is the recourse to parables. Jesus did not invent a new system for praying. Jesus was not a hermit, a Buddhist monk, or a yogi. He instead chose the daily life of his people to teach prayer with parables. This book explores the parables in the Gospels explicitly related to prayer. The reader is guided by Jesus, the original teacher of prayer with parables.

The Church in Prayer
Notes on Prayer: Volume 6
by Carthusian Monks
Carthusian Monks reside in several international monasteries. Founded in 1084 by Saint Bruno, the Order of Carthusians are dedicated to prayer, in silence, in community. Like other cloistered religious, the Carthusians live a life focused on prayer and contemplation.

The Prayer of Mary and the Saints
Notes on Prayer: Volume 7
by Catherine Aubin
When Mary appears, anywhere in the whole world, the places where she appears have points in common with the biblical places where she stayed and lived. This book reviews these places, examining what they reveal to us about Mary's identity, and what the inner spaces are that Mary asks us to dwell in today. This book also explores the unique relationship two holy women each had with Mary, leading us toward a new, deep revelation of Mary's closeness to each of us.

The Prayer Jesus Taught Us: The "Our Father"
Notes on Prayer: Volume 8
by Hugh Vanni
This book identifies the theological-biblical structure underlying the Lord's Prayer and situates it in the living environment of the early Church. This will give us a framework of reference, and as a result we will see first the antecedents in Mark, then the systematic presentation of Matthew, Paul's push forward, the accentuation of Luke, and, finally, the mature synthesis found in John.